Presidents of the United States

Presidents of the United States

Christopher Chant

GALLERY BOOKS
An imprint of W. H. Smith Publishers Inc.
112 Madison Avenue
New York, New York 10016

Photographic acknowledgments
Brian Trodd Publishing House Ltd: 35;
King/Frank Spooner Pictures: 54; Library of
Congress: 10, 12, 14, 17, 18, 22, 24, 25, 29, 31,
32, 33, 35, 37, 39, 42, 43; TRH Pictures/
Department of Defense: 44, 52.

First published in the United States of
America by
GALLERY BOOKS
An imprint of W.H. Smith Publishers Inc.
112 Madison Avenue
New York, New York 10016

ISBN 0-8317-1730-0

Printed in Portugal

Contents

Introduction

When George Bush became President of the United States of America in January, 1989, he became the 41st incumbent of this office after George Washington, the military leader largely responsible for freeing the 13 original colonies from Britain and thus paving the way for the creation of the U.S.A. and a sovereign nation.

The office of president is a uniquely powerful one, and its primary responsibility is the "faithful execution of the laws" passed by the two houses of the U.S. Congress. The creation of the office reflects the fears of the "Founding Fathers" of the American republic. They felt that abuse of power was best prevented by a dual exercise of power by Congress with its two houses of elected congressmen and senators, and by an elected president who would have very extensive powers. The president has command of the armed forces, conducts foreign affairs, has the right of veto over all congressional legislation, and appoints federal judges and other officials. However, this presidential power is balanced by constitutional safeguards: Congress has the sole right to declare war, can overturn a presidential veto by a two-thirds majority of both houses, and, as an ultimate sanction, can impeach a president for any malfeasance while in office.

For the election of the president, the Constitution of the U.S.A. ordains an electoral college, whose members are selected on a state basis to reflect the popular vote in each state. By avoiding a direct popular election for president, the originators of the Constitution hoped to remove the threat of a demagogue seizing power by his hold over the popular vote, and to prevent power blocs from manipulating the system in the same way.

There was originally no limit on the number of four-year presidential terms any one man could serve, but most presidents followed Washington's lead in serving a maximum of two terms. However, Franklin D. Roosevelt was elected to third and fourth terms, and in 1951 the Constitution was amended to make sure that no one could be elected president more than twice.

The Capitol is home to the U.S. Congress, the legislative body established by the U.S. constitution to be a popularly elected check on the president's administrative arm of the government.

DECLARATION OF INDEPENDENCE

In Congress 4th July. 1776.

A Declaration by the Representatives of the UNITED STATES OF AMERICA, in General Congress assembled.

When in the course of human events it becomes necessary for one people to dissolve the political bands which have connected them with another, and to assume among the powers of the earth the separate and equal station to which the laws of nature & of nature's god entitle them, a decent respect to the opinions of mankind requires that they should declare the causes which impel them to the separation.

We hold these truths to be self-evident; that all men are created equal & independent; that from that equal creation they derive rights inherent & inalienable, among which are the preservation of life & liberty & the pursuit of happiness; that to secure these ends, governments are instituted among men, deriving their just powers from the consent of the governed; that whenever any form of government becomes destructive of these ends, it is the right of the people to alter or to abolish it, & to institute new government, laying its foundation on such principles & organising its powers in such form, as to them shall seem most likely to effect their safety & happiness. prudence indeed will dictate that governments long established should not be changed for light & transient causes: and accordingly all experience hath shewn that mankind are more disposed to suffer while evils are sufferable, than to right themselves by abolishing the forms to which they are accustomed. but when a long train of abuses & usurpations begun at a distinguished period & pursuing invariably the same object, evinces a design to reduce them under absolute despotism, it is their right, it is their duty, to throw off such government & to provide new guards for their future security. such has been the patient sufferance of these colonies; & such is now the necessity which constrains them to expunge their former systems of government. the history of the present king of Great Britain is a history of unremitting injuries and usurpations, among which appears no solitary fact to contradict the uniform tenor of the rest, all of which have in direct object the establishment of an absolute tyranny over these states. to prove this, let facts be submitted to a candid world, for the truth of which we pledge a faith yet unsullied by falsehood.

he has refused his assent to laws the most wholesome and necessary for the public good.

he has forbidden his governors to pass laws of immediate & pressing importance, unless suspended in their operation till his assent should be obtained; and when so suspended, he has neglected utterly to attend to them.

he has refused to pass other laws for the accommodation of large districts of people, unless those people would relinquish the right of representation, a right inestimable to them, & formidable to tyrants only.

he has called together legislative bodies at places unusual, uncomfortable & distant from the depository of their public records, for the sole purpose of fatiguing them into compliance with his measures.

he has dissolved Representative houses repeatedly & continually for opposing with manly firmness his invasions on the rights of the people.

he has refused for a long time after such dissolutions to cause others to be elected;

whereby the legislative powers, incapable of annihilation, have returned to the people at large for their exercise; the state remaining in the mean time exposed to all the dangers of invasion from without, & convulsions within.

he has endeavored to prevent the population of these states; for that purpose obstructing the laws for naturalization of foreigners; refusing to pass others to encourage their migrations hither, & raising the conditions of new appropriations of lands.

he has suffered the administration of justice totally to cease in some of these states, refusing his assent to laws for establishing judiciary powers.

he has made our judges dependant on his will alone, for the tenure of their offices, and amount of their salaries.

he has erected a multitude of new offices by a self-assumed power, & sent hither swarms of officers to harass our people & eat out their substance.

he has kept among us in times of peace standing armies & ships of war without the consent of our legislatures.

he has affected to render the military independent of & superior to the civil power.

he has combined with others to subject us to a jurisdiction foreign to our constitutions and unacknowledged by our laws; giving his assent to their pretended acts of legislation, for quartering large bodies of armed troops among us;

for protecting them by a mock trial from punishment for any murders which they should commit on the inhabitants of these states;

for cutting off our trade with all parts of the world;

for imposing taxes on us without our consent;

for depriving us of the benefits of trial by jury;

for transporting us beyond seas to be tried for pretended offences:

for abolishing the free system of English laws in a neighboring province, establishing therein an arbitrary government and enlarging its boundaries, so as to render it at once an example and fit instrument for introducing the same absolute rule into these states.

for taking away our charters, & altering fundamentally the forms of our governments;

for suspending our own legislatures & declaring themselves invested with power to legislate for us in all cases whatsoever.

he has abdicated government here, withdrawing his governors, & declaring us out of his allegiance & protection.

he has plundered our seas, ravaged our coasts, burnt our towns & destroyed the lives of our people.

he is at this time transporting large armies of foreign mercenaries to compleat the works of death, desolation & tyranny, already begun with circumstances of cruelty & perfidy unworthy the head of a civilized nation.

he has endeavored to bring on the inhabitants of our frontiers the merciless Indian savages, whose known rule of warfare is an undistinguished destruction of all ages, sexes, & conditions of existence.

he has incited treasonable insurrections of our fellow-citizens, with the allurements of forfeiture & confiscation of our property.

he has waged cruel war against human nature itself, violating its most sacred rights of life & liberty in the persons of a distant people who never offended him, captivating & carrying them into slavery in another hemisphere, or to incur miserable death in their transportation thither. this piratical warfare, the opprobrium of infidel powers, is the warfare of the Christian king of Great Britain determined to keep open a market where MEN should be bought & sold he has prostituted his negative for suppressing every legislative attempt to prohibit or to restrain this execrable commerce. and that this assemblage of horrors might want no fact of distinguished die, he is now exciting those very people to rise in arms among us, and to purchase that liberty of which he has deprived them, by murdering the people upon whom he also obtruded them; thus paying off former crimes committed against the liberties of one people, with crimes which he urges them to commit against the lives of another.

in every stage of these oppressions we have petitioned for redress in the most humble terms; our repeated petitions have been answered only by repeated injuries. a prince whose character is thus marked by every act which may define a tyrant, is unfit to be the ruler of a people who mean to be free. future ages will scarce believe that the hardiness of one man adventured within the short compass of twelve years only, to build a foundation so broad & undisguised for tyranny over a people fostered & fixed in principles of freedom.

Nor have we been wanting in attentions to our British brethren. we have warned them from time to time of attempts by their legislature to extend a jurisdiction over these our states. we have reminded them of the circumstances of our emigration & settlement here, no one of which could warrant so strange a pretension: that these were effected at the expence of our own blood & treasure, unassisted by the wealth or the strength of Great Britain: that in constituting indeed our several forms of government, we had adopted one common king, thereby laying a foundation for perpetual league & amity with them: but that submission to their parliament was no part of our constitution, nor ever in idea, if history may be credited: and we appealed to their native justice & magnanimity, as well as to the ties of our common kindred to disavow these usurpations which were likely to interrupt our connection & correspondence. they too have been deaf to the voice of justice & of consanguinity. & when occasions have been given them by the regular course of their laws of removing from their councils the disturbers of our harmony, they have by their free election re-established them in power. at this very time too they are permitting their chief magistrate to send over not only soldiers of our common blood, but Scotch & foreign mercenaries to invade & destroy us. these facts have given the last stab to agonizing affection, and manly spirit bids us to renounce for ever these unfeeling brethren. we must endeavor to forget our former love for them, and to hold them as we hold the rest of mankind, enemies in war, in peace friends. we might have been a free & a great people together; but a communication of grandeur & of freedom it seems is below their dignity. be it so, since they will have it: the road to happiness & to glory is open to us too; we will tread it apart from them, and acquiesce in the necessity which denounces our eternal separation!

We therefore the representatives of the United States of America in General Congress assembled, do in the name, & by authority of the good people of these states reject and renounce all allegiance & subjection to the kings of Great Britain & all others who may hereafter claim by, through, or under them; we utterly dissolve all political connection which may heretofore have subsisted between us & the people or parliament of Great Britain: and finally we do assert and declare these colonies to be free and independent states, and that as free & independent states they shall hereafter have power to levy war, conclude peace, contract alliances, establish commerce, & to do all other acts and things which independent states may of right do. And for the support of this declaration we mutually pledge to each other our lives, our fortunes, & our sacred honour.

John Hancock   Saml Lewis   Rich Stockton   Carter Braxton   Arthur Middleton   Step Hopkins   Th Jefferson

Wm Whipple   Casar Rodney   George Wythe   Benj Harrison   Th Nelson

Rob Morris   John Penn   Samuel Chase   John Hart   Geo Read   Richard Henry Lee   John Adams

Benjamin Rush   Wm Paca   Tho Stone   Abra Clark   Tho M Kean   Josiah Bartlett   Matthew Thornton   Roger Sherman

Benj Franklin   Geo Taylor   Geo Ross   Edward Rutledge   Sam Huntington   William Ellery   Charles Carroll of Carrollton

Joseph Hewes   Wm Floyd   Phil Livingston   Jns Witherspoon   Button Gwinnett   Thos Heyward Jun   Geo Clymer   Wm Williams   Robt Treat Paine

Wm Hooper   Lyman Hall   Thomas Lynch Jun   Lewis Morris   Ja Smith   Oliver Wolcott   Elbridge Gerry

John Morton   James Wilson   Fras Hopkinson   Geo Walton   Sam Adams

9

George Washington
1st President

As the colonies became disenchanted with British rule, Washington was selected as a Virginia delegate to the Continental Congress. In June, 1775, he was appointed to command of the Continental Army. Washington's great achievement in this task was the maintenance of American unity until the colonial army eventually won its victory in 1783.

Somewhat unwillingly, Washington was persuaded to stand unopposed for president, but was unable to carry this unifying capability into his political career. His administration was deeply divided by the ambitions of his two principal appointees: Thomas Jefferson, the

On 30 April 1779 George Washington became the first American president in New York, temporary capital of the United States. He had been elected without opposition by the unanimous 69-0 vote of the Electoral College. The tasks imposed on this modest man were enormous: much of the "civilized world" expected him to preside over a country that would descend into chaos with popular government, while the rest thought that he would find despotism the only alternative to popular chaos. Yet, in his two terms, Washington rode so true a line between the pitfalls that he established the presidency on a secure footing and secured for himself the accolade "Father of the Republic".

Washington was born into an affluent Virginia family, and eventually inherited an estate which he increased to 100,000 acres. Washington embarked on a military career in 1753, but in 1759 he married a wealthy widow, Martha Dandridge Custis, and became increasingly involved in plantation management.

Secretary of State, disapproved of the strong central government advocated by Alexander Hamilton, the Secretary of the Treasury. Washington was re-elected unopposed in 1792, and the highlights of his administrations may be regarded as the move of the capital to Philadelphia in 1790, the adoption of the Bill of Rights in 1791, and the creation of the Bank of the United States in 1792. His second term was less successful in overall terms, but marked the emergence of a strong Federalist tendency, exaggerated by Jefferson's resignation in 1793. Washington's celebrated "Farewell Address" of 1796 stressed the need for unity, and in March, 1797, Washington retired to his estate at Mount Vernon, where he died, in December, 1799.

Opposite: *The celebrated cherry tree episode from Washington's childhood.*
Above left: *Washington's home at Mount Vernon, Virginia.*
Above: *Retreating before the British in 1776, Washington crosses the Delaware to the temporary safety of Pennsylvania.*

Birthplace	Bridges Creek, Virginia
Date of Birth	22 February 1732
Education	Common schools
Profession	Planter and soldier
Presidential term	30 April 1789 to 4 March 1797
Party	no party in his first term, and Federalist in his second
Place of death	Mount Vernon, Virginia
Date of death	14 December 1799
Place of burial	Mount Vernon, Virginia

John Adams
2nd President

John Adams

After two terms as Washington's vice-president, John Adams became president in 1796 after defeating the Democrat-Republican Thomas Jefferson, 71 Electoral College votes to 68. Trained as a lawyer, Adams played a prominent part in the events leading up to the War of Independence and was a delegate to the Continental Congress. During the war Adams was a commissioner to France, and after the war served as U.S. Ambassador to the Netherlands and then to Great Britain. Adams was selected to stand against Jefferson in 1796 only because the Federalists considered Hamilton too controversial a candidate. The Adams administration was generally undistinguished, but was notable for the move of the capital to a new site on the Potomac river chosen by (and named for) Washington, and a steady deterioration in relations with France. Despite attacks by French privateers on U.S. shipping and the war-mongering tendency in many members of his own party, Adams resisted the drift to war. In 1800 he reached an agreement with France. Adams lived quietly in retirement from 1801.

The Declaration of Independence is one of history's most important documents, but its wording was agreed only after lengthy debate.

Birthplace	Braintree (now Quincy), Massachusetts
Date of birth	30 October 1735
Education	Harvard
Profession	Lawyer
Presidential term	4 March 1797 to 4 March 1801
Party	Federalist
Place of death	Braintree (now Quincy), Massachusetts
Date of death	4 July 1826
Place of burial	Braintree (now Quincy), Massachusetts

Thomas Jefferson
3rd President

Birthplace	Shadwell, Virginia
Date of birth	13 April 1743
Education	College of William and Mary
Profession	Lawyer
Presidential term	4 March 1801 to 4 March 1809
Party	Democrat-Republican
Place of death	Monticello, Virginia
Date of death	4 July 1826
Place of burial	Monticello, Virginia

The Jefferson Memorial is a fitting monument to a man who was undoubtedly one of the finest presidents ever possessed by the U.S.

Thomas Jefferson was a truly remarkable man. One of the main authors of the Declaration of Independence, he was a champion of decentralized democracy, and a president who virtually doubled the size of the United States. In addition, he was also an agriculturist, archaeologist, architect, geographer, meteorologist, musician, palaeontologist, and scientist—among other things.

At the age of 14 Jefferson inherited his father's tobacco plantation in Virginia. He would have preferred a scientific career, but opted instead for the law and qualified in 1767. In 1769 he entered the Virginia House of Burgesses, and as a delegate to the Continental Congress in 1775 was appointed to the committee overseeing the drafting of the Declaration of Independence. Between 1776 and 1789 Jefferson was prominent in local, national, and even international politics. He then became Washington's Secretary of State until 1793. He was defeated by Adams in the 1796 election, but by a strange quirk secured the vice-

Among other accomplishments Jefferson was an architect, and in Washington he designed the internationally celebrated Library of Congress.

presidency because of divided Federalist loyalties for Adams' running mate.

Riding a crest of anti-Federalist sentiment in the election of 1800, Jefferson tied with the Democrat-Republican Aaron Burr. Both men secured 73 Electoral College votes, and the House of Representatives finally voted for Jefferson. Surer victory was secured in 1804, when Jefferson defeated the Federalist Charles Pinckney by 162 votes to 14. The keystones of Jefferson's administration were the imposition of a strict political neutrality on the judiciary, the abolition of internal taxation, the reduction of the armed forces, and the enhancement of states' rights at the expense of the federal union. At the time of Jefferson's election, the

U.S.A. reached as far west as the Mississippi River, but the astute president took advantage of Europe's embroilment in war to secure the "Louisiana Purchase" in 1803. For $15 million, the U.S.A. bought from France some 1 million square miles of territory between the Mississippi and the Rocky Mountains. Other features of Jefferson's presidency were piracy-inspired war with the Barbary states, the Lewis and Clark expedition to the Pacific coast, the 1807 Embargo Act attempting to halt foreign trade in an effort to prevent accusations of favouritism that might force the U.S.A. to join one side or the other in the Napoleonic wars, and the 1808 prohibition of slave importation. After his retirement Jefferson lived quietly.

Born to a land-owning family in Virginia, James Madison is remembered as the president responsible for the War of 1812, known as "Mr. Madison's War". A member of the Continental Congress, he then took a major part in the Annapolis and Philadelphia Conventions that created the Constitution. He became a congressman in 1789, and proposed the first 10 amendments that became the basis of the Bill of Rights. Madison later became Jefferson's Secretary of State, and played an important role in the Louisiana Purchase. With Jefferson's retirement Madison succeeded him as president, with 122 Electoral College votes to the Federalist Charles Pinckney's 47; in the 1812 election Madison secured 128 votes to the Federalist DeWitt Clinton's 89. Madison inherited Jefferson's problems with European trade, and faced Indian opposition to further settlement in the west. Believing Britain to be behind both difficulties, Madison persuaded Congress to declare war in 1812. Before peace was restored in 1814, the British had burned Washington and its new presidential residence, the White House.

James Madison
4th President

Birthplace	Port Conway, Virginia
Date of birth	16 March 1751
Education	College of New Jersey (later Princeton)
Profession	Lawyer
Presidential term	4 March 1809 to 4 March 1817
Party	Democrat-Republican
Place of death	Montpelier, Virginia
Date of death	28 June 1826
Place of burial	Montpelier, Virginia

The War of 1812 was notable for a series of American-won single-ship actions such as this between USS Constitution *and HMS* Guerriere.

James Monroe
5th President

James Monroe [signature]

The White House was so nicknamed for the white paint applied after it had been burned by the British in the War of 1812.

James Monroe fought in the War of Independence and then studied law under Jefferson, who persuaded him to enter political life, first in the Virginia House of Delegates and then as a congressman and senator. After ambassadorial posts in France, Spain and Britain, he returned to the U.S., and between 1811 and 1817 was Madison's Secretary of State and then Secretary of War. In the 1816 election Monroe defeated the Federalist Rufus King with 183 Electoral College votes to 34, and in the 1820 election he secured 231 votes to the Democrat-Republican John Quincy Adams's 1. Monroe moved into the restored "White House", and his presidency was an untroubled period that saw the U.S. rise to great prosperity. The Rush-Bagott Agreement of 1817 effectively demilitarized the Great Lakes, the Missouri Compromise of 1820 banned slavery in the Louisiana Purchase north of 36° 30' North, and Florida was ceded by Spain in 1821. But this president is best remembered for the "Monroe Doctrine" whereby the U.S. consistently refused for decades to interfere in the internal affairs of other countries in the Americas. Monroe retired in 1825 and lived the rest of his life in financial difficulties.

Birthplace	Monroe's Creek, Virginia
Date of birth	28 April 1758
Education	College of William and Mary
Profession	Lawyer
Presidential term	4 March 1817 to 4 March 1825
Party	Democrat-Republican
Place of death	New York, New York
Date of death	4 July 1831
Place of burial	Richmond, Virginia

The foundation in Washington of the Smithsonian Institution was a major achievement of the presidency of John Quincy Adams.

Birthplace	Braintree (now Quincy), Massachusetts
Date of birth	11 July 1767
Education	Harvard
Profession	Lawyer
Presidential term	4 March 1825 to 4 March 1829
Party	National Republican
Place of death	Washington, D.C.
Date of death	23 February 1848
Place of burial	Braintree (now Quincy), Massachusetts

John Quincy Adams
6th President

John Quincy Adams was the son of the second president. He is seen as a great American statesman, able with a far-sighted vision of the U.S. as a continental power. At the same time he is regarded as an inept president. As a young man, Adams accompanied his father to Europe, and studied law before becoming U.S. Ambassador to the Netherlands and Prussia. He entered politics as a Federalist, but then became a Democrat-Republican. He served as Madison's ambassador to Russia and Britain, and then as Monroe's Secretary of State. Adams was largely responsible for Monroe's territorial gains, including the 1819 Transcontinental Treaty that extended the Louisiana Purchase's western frontier to the Pacific. In 1825 Adams ran as a National-Republican and came second with 84 votes to the Democrat Andrew Jackson with 99 votes. In the absence of a clear majority the decision was put to the House of Representatives and the fourth contestant gave Adams his votes. His term was marked by obstruction by Jackson's adherents, and he lost in 1828 after a very dirty campaign.

Andrew Jackson
7th President

Andrew Jackson (signature)

The first presidential "man of the people", Andrew Jackson fought against the British in the War of Independence and then studied law. Successful as a lawyer and local politician, Jackson was also an effective Indian fighter, and beat the British in the 1814 Battle of New Orleans. Defeated in the 1824 presidential election, Jackson fought in 1828 as a Democrat and triumphed with 178 Electoral College votes to Adams's 83. In 1832 his opponent was the Democrat-Republican Henry Clay,

and Jackson won with 219 to 49 votes.

Jackson's administration was a studied combination of the larger-than-life with the homespun. He favoured a cabinet of loyal supporters among whom only Martin Van Buren, vice-president from 1833 to 1837, had any real ability. Key events of Jackson's presidency were the Black Hawk War of 1832, the Nullification Crisis in which Jackson used the threat of federal strength to crush the right of a state—South Carolina—to refuse federal law, the destruction of the Bank of the United States, the split of the Democrat-Republican party into Jackson's Democrats and Clay's National-Republicans, the nomination of presidential candidates by national conventions rather than congressional caucuses, the recognition of Texas' independence from Mexico, and the Panic of 1837, which undermined his popularity.

Birthplace	Waxhaw Settlement, South Carolina
Date of birth	15 March 1757
Education	Self-educated
Profession	Lawyer and soldier
Presidential term	4 March 1829 to 4 March 1837
Party	Democrat
Place of death	Hermitage, Tennessee
Date of death	8 June 1845
Place of burial	Hermitage, Tennessee

The Battle of New Orleans in January 1915 was a crushing British defeat, and was fought by the Americans under the command of Andrew Jackson.

Birthplace	Kinderhook, New York
Date of birth	5 December 1782
Education	Common schools
Profession	Lawyer
Presidential term	4 March 1837 to 4 March 1841
Party	Democrat
Place of death	Kinderhook, New York
Date of death	24 July 1862
Place of burial	Kinderhook, New York

Martin Van Buren
8th President

Martin Van Buren became a New York state senator in 1812, and moved to the U.S. Senate in 1827. In 1829 he became Governor of New York, but resigned to become Secretary of State in Jackson's first administration. In 1833 he became vice-president in Jackson's second administration, and was thus well placed for the 1836 presidential election. He stood as a Democrat and secured 170 Electoral College votes to the Whig General William Harrison's 73. Van Buren took office at the time when Jackson's financial "reforms" were having their most dire results. A land boom fuelled by paper money collapsed and the U.S. entered a period of depression, partially lifted in 1838 and then exacerbated by a skimpy grain harvest and the crash of cotton prices. Van Buren refused to panic and secured the passing of the 1840 Independent Treasury Act, which removed all connection between banks and the federal government. Van Buren can also be credited with the creation of the modern American electioneering system, but fell foul of his own brainchild in 1840 and failed to win re-election.

The early part of the 19th century was notable for a rapid expansion westward by settlers amongst the U.S.A.'s rapidly growing population.

William H. Harrison
9th President

W H Harrison

Birthplace	Berkeley, Virginia
Date of birth	9 February 1773
Education	Hampden-Sidney
Profession	Soldier
Presidential term	4 March 1841 to 4 April 1841
Party	Whig
Place of death	Washington, D.C.
Date of death	4 April 1841
Place of burial	North Bend, Ohio

William Henry Harrison has the unusual distinction of having been the first president to die in office, and also the man to hold the presidency for the shortest time. Harrison entered the army in 1791. In 1798 he resigned the service to become Secretary to the Northwest Territory, and he was territorial delegate to Congress one year later. However, it was as Governor of the Indiana territory that Harrison made his name: having allowed white settlers to overwhelm the Indians, Harrison crushed the inevitable Shawnee uprising under Tecumseh in the Battle of Tippecanoe during 1811, and was promoted to Major General in the War of 1812. In the next 20 years he was a congressman and senator. Running against Van Buren in 1836, he proved a popular candidate for his plain military bearing rather than any particular policies. Capitalizing on Van Buren's unpopularity, Harrison ran again in 1840 and won soundly with 234 Electoral College votes to 60. As his supporters squabbled for power under the Harrison figurehead, "Old Tip" died 31 days after taking office.

The single event that made Harrison a household name was his success against Tecumseh in the Battle of Tippecanoe during 1811.

Birthplace	Greenway, Virginia
Date of birth	29 March 1790
Education	College of William and Mary
Profession	Lawyer
Presidential term	4 April 1841 to 4 March 1845
Party	Whig
Place of death	Richmond, Virginia
Date of death	18 January 1862
Place of burial	Richmond, Virginia

John Tyler
10th President

John Tyler

With Harrison's death the mantle of president fell on his vice-president, John Tyler. It was the first time in American history that a man had claimed the presidency through right of succession. Tyler, an erstwhile member of the Democrat party, had been chosen to run with Harrison in an effort to create a balanced ticket. On his accession to the presidency, he therefore lacked the support of a firmly committed party machine behind him. He was castigated by the Democrats and then fell foul of the Whig party in the Congress, headed by Henry Clay. Tyler's background was typical of a politician of his time: he had been a member of the Virginia House of Delegates, Congress and the Virginia legislature before becoming Governor of Virginia in 1825-26 and a senator in 1827-36. Highlights of Tyler's administration were the repeal of the Independent Treasury Act, the settlement of the second Seminole war, the agreement of the U.S. Canadian frontier between Maine and New Brunswick, and the annexation of Texas. In September 1841 his entire cabinet but one resigned, and Tyler thereafter ruled without any party backing. He was persuaded not to stand for election in 1844.

Under Osceola the Seminoles of Georgia and Florida fought the 2nd Seminole War (1835-43) to avoid the tribe's forcible removal west.

James K. Polk
11th President

James Polk was a lawyer and politician who served in the Tennessee legislature and in Congress before becoming Speaker and Governor of Tennessee. He was a firm believer in the "Manifest Destiny" of the United States to occupy the North American continent. It was this factor that persuaded the Democrats to nominate Polk as their candidate against the Whigs' Henry Clay. Polk won the election with 170 to 105 Electoral College votes, though the difference in the 2.7-million popular vote was only

Birthplace	Mecklenburg County, North Carolina
Date of birth	2 November 1795
Eduction	University of North Carolina
Profession	Lawyer
Presidential term	4 March 1845 to 4 March 1849
Party	Democrat
Place of death	Nashville, Tennessee
Date of death	15 June 1849
Place of burial	Nashville, Tennessee

38,000. Polk's expansionist platform soon began to pay dividends: Texas was admitted to statehood, and Britain yielded its portion of Oregon to the U.S. Mexico meanwhile declared war over the Texas issue, and the Mexican War was not brought to a successful conclusion until 1848, when the Treaty of Guadalupe Hidalgo established the Mexican/U.S. border along the Rio Grande and brought California and New Mexico into the union. Polk refused nomination for a second term.

Of immense social, political and economic importance in Polk's presidency was the discovery of gold in California, leading to the 1849 "gold rush".

Birthplace	Orange County, Virginia
Date of birth	24 November 1784
Education	Self-educated
Profession	Soldier
Presidential term	4 March 1849 to 9 July 1850
Party	Whig
Place of death	Washington, D.C.
Date of death	9 July 1850
Place of burial	Louisville, Kentucky

Zachary Taylor
12th President

Zachary Taylor was elevated to the presidency almost exclusively by the popularity he won as one of the two major field commanders of the U.S. forces in the Mexican War of 1846-48, both staunch Whigs. The Democrat Polk tried to keep the war to a level small enough to raise neither man in public esteem, but large enough to warrant a peace treaty that would yield the U.S. significant gains. Yet Taylor was nominated as the Whig candidate and prevailed over the Democrat Lewis Cass by 163 Electoral College votes to 127. Taylor had no experience of political life, and offered the country a non-partisan administration centred on statehood for New Mexico and California. Both would be free to choose to be slave or free states. The inevitability of their choice as free states incensed the slave-owning southern states, who accurately foresaw the upset of their current balance with the free northern states. Taylor did not have to face the problem, for he died of typhus after only 16 months in office.

Zachary Taylor made his name as the U.S. commanding general in the Mexican War (1846-48), and rode the resultant popularity into the White House.

Millard Fillmore
13th President

Millard Fillmore [signature]

By Fillmore's presidency slavery was already a highly emotive factor the most obvious feature of the main issue, individual states' rights.

After Taylor's death the vice-president, the ineffective Millard Fillmore, became president. Buying himself out of apprenticeship to a clothier, Fillmore studied law. After six years as a lawyer he turned to politics, where he served in the New York legislature before becoming a congressman. As president, Fillmore managed Congress better than Taylor had. He was able to smooth the way for the passing in September 1850 of the so-called "Compromise Measures": California was admitted as a free state, New Mexico and Utah became territories with no limitations on slavery, the Texas boundary was fixed, the slave trade was abolished in Washington, D.C., and a stricter fugitive slave law was enacted. However, Fillmore's measures failed to satisfy either side and his popularity plummeted. The only other noteworthy event of the Fillmore administration was the despatch of Commodore Perry's expedition to open relations with Japan. Fillmore failed to secure party nomination for presidential candidature in 1852.

Birthplace	Cayuga County, New York
Date of birth	7 January 1800
Education	Self-educated
Profession	Lawyer
Presidential term	9 July 1850 to 4 March 1853
Party	Whig
Place of death	Buffalo, New York
Date of death	8 March 1874
Place of burial	Buffalo, New York

Photography proved a potent tool in the abolitionists' cause to "prove" the mistreatment of slaves in the slave-owning states of the south.

Franklin Pierce
14th President

Franklin Pierce was a wholly ineffectual president of personal but limited charm. The tragedy of his term is that the U.S. was drifting with remorseless momentum towards civil war, and a succession of poor presidents was unable even to slow this drift. Pierce was born into a political family, and after training as a lawyer moved into politics through the standard channel of the New Hampshire legislature, the House of Representatives and the Senate. After fighting in the Mexican War, Pierce was the Democrat presidential candidate in 1852 and defeated the Whig General Winfield Scott by 254 Electoral College votes to 42. The only highlights of his career were the Gadsden Purchase, in which 45,000 square miles of territory were bought from Mexico for $10 million, and the ill-conceived Kansas-Nebraska Act, which opened the two territories to settlement and self-determination on the slavery issue north of the line ordained in the 1820 Missouri Compromise. The result was a revival of the Whigs as the Republican party, and Pierce failed to secure re-nomination in 1856.

Birthplace	Hillsboro, New Hampshire
Date of birth	23 November 1804
Education	Bowdoin
Profession	Lawyer
Presidential term	4 March 1853 to 4 March 1857
Party	Democrat
Place of death	Concord, New Hampshire
Date of death	8 October 1869
Place of burial	Concord, New Hampshire

James Buchanan
15th President

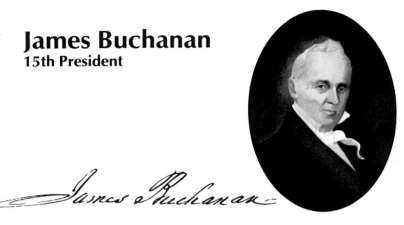

[signature: James Buchanan]

One of the men who helped spark off the Civil War was the anti-slavery campaigner John Brown, hanged with six others for treason in March 1860.

Much was expected of James Buchanan, a highly experienced and apparently able politician. As president, however, he proved too pliable in the hands of his advisers and lacked the strength of character to resist the arguments of a cabinet increasingly dominated by southerners: it was in the last months of Buchanan's presidency that the Confederacy came into being. After early service in the Pennsylvania legislature and Congress, Buchanan became Jackson's ambassador to Russia, Polk's Secretary of State and the same president's ambassador to Britain. For the 1856 election Buchanan secured the Democrat nomination, securing 174 Electoral College votes to the Republican John C. Fremont's 114. Buchanan's term was notable for a steady succession of pro-southern measures and court rulings. Abraham Lincoln's victory in the 1860 election prompted the secession from the union of South Carolina. That state was soon joined by other southern states in a move Buchanan felt himself powerless to oppose.

Birthplace	Franklin County, Pennsylvania
Date of Birth	23 April 1791
Education	Dickinson College
Profession	Lawyer
Presidential term	4 March 1857 to 4 March 1861
Party	Democrat
Place of death	Lancaster, Pennsylvania
Date of death	1 June 1868
Place of burial	Lancaster, Pennsylvania

A highlight of Abraham Lincoln's presidency was the Emancipation Proclamation that became law only after Lincoln's death.

Abraham Lincoln
16th President

Abraham Lincoln

One of the truly great presidents, Abraham Lincoln presided over the grim years of the Civil War, yet was also able to lay the foundations of the post-war reconciliation. There is no doubt that Lincoln was an extremely complex character, and he was also an exceptionally able politician, able to tailor his public thoughts and speeches to the requirements of the moment. Born into a poor family and brought up largely on the frontier, Lincoln developed into a capable outdoorsman and served in the Black Hawk War. He then taught himself law, and in 1847 became a Whig congressman for Illinois. The matter that finally brought Lincoln to the fore was slavery: he was not an abolitionist as such, but he saw slavery as a morally abhorrent condition. He made a celebrated speech against the Kansas-Nebraska Bill promoted by Stephen A. Douglas. Lincoln then joined the Republican party, and campaigned in a high-profile but unsuccessful manner against Douglas for a senatorial seat.

Lincoln's great eloquence against Douglas persuaded

This illustration of the Battle of the Wilderness (5-6 May 1864) stylizes the terrible savagery of many Civil War battles, when the southern secessionist states of the Confederacy were ground down by the manpower and industrial resources of the Unionist states of the north.

the Republicans to nominate him for president in 1860 on a platform of anti-slavery in the territories. With the opposition divided between northern and southern Democrat factions and a Constitutional Union candidate, Lincoln won a clear victory with 180 Electoral College votes against the 72 of his nearest rival, the southern Democrat John C. Breckinridge. Lincoln's election made southern secession inevitable, and with it the near certainty of civil war. During the Civil War of 1861-65, Lincoln managed to keep the British from becoming involved, appointed Ulysses S. Grant as the highly effective commander of the union forces, and co-ordinated the north's efforts, both industrial and organizational, that secured Union victory.

In 1863 Lincoln promulgated measures for slave emancipation, and in 1864 won re-election with 212 Electoral College votes to the Democrat George B. McClellan's 21. The war ended just after he finished his first term, and only a few days after his inauguration to a second, he was shot by John Wilkes Booth, an actor who favored the southern cause. Lincoln died the following

Birthplace	Hardin County (now Larue County), Kentucky
Date of birth	12 February 1809
Education	Self-educated
Profession	Lawyer
Presidential term	4 March 1861 to 15 April 1865
Party	Republican
Place of death	Washington, D.C.
Date of death	15 April 1865
Place of burial	Springfield, Illinois

A capable man with an unfortunate chip on his shoulder because of his humble birth, Andrew Johnson succeeded from the vice-presidency to the presidency with the assassination of Lincoln. Johnson was the only southern senator to adhere to the unionist cause in the Civil War, and he was nominated for vice-president in the 1864 election to secure a balanced ticket. Highlights of his presidential career were the ratification of the 13th Amendment abolishing slavery and the Alaska Purchase, in which the whole of Alaska was bought from Russia for $7.2 million. Johnson followed the conciliatory post-war policies of Lincoln, but fell foul of Congress for vetoing legislation in which Congress sought to restore black rights limited by southern state legislation. Johnson finally dismissed Edwin Stanton, the Secretary of War, who wished to use the army to promote black rights in the south. This action led to his impeachment, which finally failed by a single vote. An embittered Johnson refused to seek re-election.

Andrew Johnson
17th President

Birthplace	Raleigh, North Carolina
Date of birth	29 December 1808
Education	Self-educated
Profession	Tailor
Presidential term	15 April 1865 to 4 March 1869
Party	Democrat/Republican
Place of death	Carter's Station, Tennessee
Date of death	31 July 1875
Place of burial	Greenville, Tennessee

Only one president has been impeached, the proceedings against Johnson beginning on 13 March 1868 and failing by a single vote.

Ulysses S. Grant
18th President

Birthplace	Point Pleasant, Ohio
Date of birth	27 April 1822
Education	U.S. Military Academy, West Point
Profession	Soldier
Presidential term	4 March 1869 to 4 March 1877
Party	Republican
Place of death	Mt. McGregor, New York
Date of death	23 July 1885
Place of burial	New York, New York

Ulysses S. Grant will be remembered as a great general but a poor president. He was a heavy drinker, and his eight-year term was marked by political and personal weakness and a dismal choice of advisers. After his success as commanding general of the union forces in the Civil War, Grant was appointed Secretary of War in succession to Stanton, but then fell out with Johnson and switched to the Republicans, who nominated him for the 1868 election that he won with 214 Electoral College votes to the Democrat Horatio Seymour's 80. Despite scandals about political nepotism, Grant's popularity remained high and he was re-elected in 1872 with 286 votes to the Democrat Horace Greeley's 66. Further scandals followed, as did national concern about the dire condition of the southern states where the Ku Klux Klan rose to great power. Grant did not seek re-election in 1876.

One of Grant's military highpoints was the siege of Vicksburg in 1863.

Temperance became a potent political force in the 1870s.

WOMAN'S HOLY WAR.

Rutherford B. Hayes
19th President

R. B. Hayes was an able president who should be best remembered for ending the period of "reconstruction" in the south and for his much needed reform of the civil service. In fact, he is best remembered as the winner of what was most probably the most fraudulent presidential election in American history. A lawyer who rose to the rank of major general in the Civil War, Hayes then entered politics and secured the Republicans' nomination for the 1876 election. In that contest Hayes secured 165 Electoral College votes to the Democrat Samuel J. Tilden's 184. The remaining 20 contested votes belonged to four Republican-run states, where the party apparatus rigged matters so that all 20 went to Hayes after the deliberations of a special electoral commission. The furious Democrats agreed to accept Hayes as president only if he withdrew federal troops from the southern states and left them to manage their own affairs. This helped to end the "carpetbagger" period and, at the expense of black rights, eased north/south tensions.

Birthplace	Delaware, Ohio
Date of birth	4 October 1822
Education	Kenyon and Harvard
Profession	Lawyer
Presidential term	4 March 1877 to 4 March 1881
Party	Republican
Place of death	Fremont, Ohio
Date of death	17 January 1893
Place of burial	Fremont, Ohio

James A. Garfield
20th President

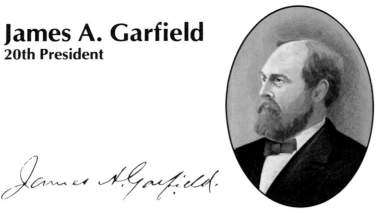

James A. Garfield (signature)

James Garfield was born to a poor farming family and worked at several jobs, including canal bargeman, before he worked his way through college. A committed Christian, Garfield entered politics in the 1850s with a firm belief against slavery. During the Civil War Garfield rose to major general, and became a senator in 1880. Garfield was the Republicans' presidential nominee in 1880 after two-thirds of the divided party united in an effort to prevent the other third securing Grant's nomination for a third term. In the election Garfield secured 214 Electoral College votes to the Democrat General Winfield Scott Hancock's 155, though the popular vote favoured Garfield by only 7,000. Garfield's early presidency was marred by party squabbles about appointments, and on 2 July 1881, after five months in office, Garfield was shot. He died several months later.

HISTORICAL PHOTOGRAPH

The presidency of James Garfield remains imponderable because he was shot only four months after taking office. This photo collage shows his assassin, the gun used, the B&P Depot where Garfield was shot and the doctors who tried to revive him.

Birthplace	Orange, Ohio
Date of birth	19 November 1831
Education	Williams College
Profession	Teacher
Presidential term	4 March 1881 to 19 September 1881
Party	Republican
Place of death	Elberon, New Jersey
Date of death	19 September 1881
Place of burial	Cleveland, Ohio

Chester A. Arthur
21th President

Chester Arthur was Garfield's vice-president solely for Republican factional purposes. A supporter of Grant, he was chosen in an effort to rally the pro-Grant "Stalwart" faction behind Garfield. With long experience in the murky waters of New York state politics, Arthur was a man of decidedly dubious reputation. However, after he became president on Garfield's death, he proved himself a conscientious and efficient administrator who did much to reform the extraordinarily corrupt civil service. The Pendleton Act reserved ten per cent of government jobs for candidates who were successful in competitive examinations supervised by a civil service commission. Arthur also fought against corruption in the postal service and successfully demanded the creation of a modern navy. But he had fallen foul of the "Stalwart" faction by these moves and failed dismally to secure re-nomination in 1884.

Typical of the U.S.A.'s growth under Arthur was Brooklyn Bridge in New York.

Birthplace	Fairfield, Vermont
Date of birth	5 October 1830
Education	Union College
Profession	Lawyer
Presidential term	19 September 1881 to 4 March 1885
Party	Republican
Place of death	New York, New York
Date of death	18 November 1886
Place of burial	Albany, New York

Grover Cleveland
22nd and 24th President

Birthplace	Caldwell, New Jersey
Date of birth	18 March 1837
Education	Common schools
Profession	Lawyer
Presidential terms	4 March 1885 to 4 March 1889
	4 March 1893 to 4 March 1897
Party	Democrat
Place of death	Princeton, New Jersey
Date of death	24 June 1908
Place of burial	Princeton, New Jersey

Grover Cleveland has the distinction of being the only president elected to two non-consecutive terms, the first Democrat president in 28 years and, by the standards of the day, a notably honest politician. After a simple education, Cleveland learned law the hard way, as an articled clerk. He made his name in local politics because of his obvious probity, and eventually became a reforming Governor of New York who cracked down on corruption. In 1884 Cleveland became the democratic nominee for president, and won a particularly dirty election with 219 Electoral College votes to the 182 secured by his Republican opponent, James G. Blaine. Cleveland's first term was notable for little except the president's marriage, which took place in the White House. Cleveland lost the 1888 election, but won in 1892 with 277 votes to 145 cast for the Republican, Benjamin Harrison. Cleveland's second administration was marked by the "gold bug" financial scare.

Frances Cleveland was at 21 the U.S.A.'s youngest first lady.

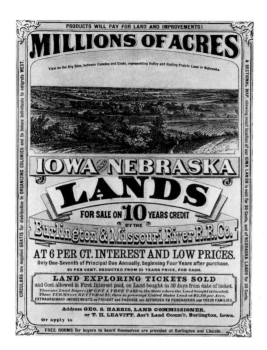

Benjamin Harrison
23rd President

The grandson of the ninth president, Benjamin Harrison must go down in history as one of the less capable presidents, a cold, but personally honest, man who won neither personal friendship nor the approval of politicians who used their power for corrupt purposes. This was a marked contrast to the situation in the two Cleveland administrations between which Harrison's term was sandwiched. Harrison was a self-taught lawyer, and reached the rank of brigadier general in the Civil War. An indifferent political career followed, and it was mainly his pedigree as William Henry's descendant that helped to secure the Republican nomination in 1888. Thanks to the efforts of big business, Harrison won with 233 Electoral College votes to the 168 of Cleveland, who took the popular vote by 100,000. Harrison's administration was notable for some important legislation, but the president himself had little to do with it.

Birthplace	North Bend, Ohio
Date of birth	20 August 1833
Education	Miami University
Profession	Lawyer
Presidential term	4 March 1889 to 4 March 1893
Party	Republican
Place of death	Indianapolis, Indiana
Date of death	13 March 1901
Place of burial	Indianapolis, Indiana

Harrison's presidency saw a major land rush to the west.

William McKinley
25th President

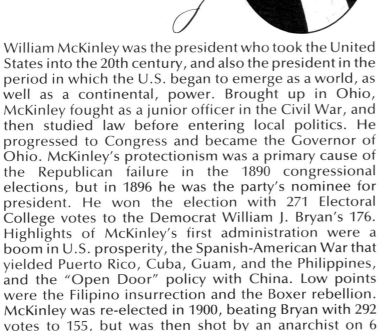

Birthplace	Niles, Ohio
Date of birth	29 January 1843
Education	Allegheny College and Albany Law School
Profession	Lawyer
Presidential term	4 March 1897 to 14 September 1901
Party	Republican
Place of death	Buffalo, New York
Date of death	14 September 1901
Place of death	Canton, Ohio

William McKinley was the president who took the United States into the 20th century, and also the president in the period in which the U.S. began to emerge as a world, as well as a continental, power. Brought up in Ohio, McKinley fought as a junior officer in the Civil War, and then studied law before entering local politics. He progressed to Congress and became the Governor of Ohio. McKinley's protectionism was a primary cause of the Republican failure in the 1890 congressional elections, but in 1896 he was the party's nominee for president. He won the election with 271 Electoral College votes to the Democrat William J. Bryan's 176. Highlights of McKinley's first administration were a boom in U.S. prosperity, the Spanish-American War that yielded Puerto Rico, Cuba, Guam, and the Philippines, and the "Open Door" policy with China. Low points were the Filipino insurrection and the Boxer rebellion. McKinley was re-elected in 1900, beating Bryan with 292 votes to 155, but was then shot by an anarchist on 6 September 1901. He died eight days later.

The explosion that blew up the battleship USS Maine also sparked the Spanish-American War (1898) that freed Cuba from Spain and gave the Philippines, Guam, and Puerto Rico to the U.S.A.

Though conceived in McKinley's presidency, it was under the driving leadership of Theodore Roosevelt that the construction of the Panama Canal was pushed forward with such phenomenal energy.

Theodore Roosevelt
26th President

Theodore Roosevelt (signature)

Theodore Roosevelt was only 42 at the time of his inauguration, and as the youngest-ever president he brought to the White House a flush of energy both physical and moral. His charisma restored to the presidency much of the prestige lost to Congress by his indifferent predecessors. Born to an affluent New York family, Roosevelt was a sickly youth to whom a robust constitution came as a result of the strenuous outdoor activity recommended by his father. The family was shocked by Roosevelt's decision to enter politics as a

Birthplace	New York, New York
Date of birth	27 October 1858
Education	Harvard and Columbia
Profession	Lawyer
Presidential term	14 September 1901 to 4 March 1909
Party	Republican
Place of death	Oyster Bay, New York
Date of death	6 January 1919
Place of burial	Oyster Bay, New York

A party poster depicts Theodore Roosevelt as the "Apostle of Prosperity". The other side of the coin was his fight against big business trusts.

The original Teddy bear made in 1903 by the Ideal Toy Company and is preserved in the Smithsonian Institution. It was so named after the publicity about "Teddy" Roosevelt's refusal to shoot a bear cub while hunting in November 1902.

Republican in the state legislature, but after only three years he resigned to become a rancher in North Dakota after the death within 24 hours of his mother and wife.

Two years later Roosevelt returned, remarried and once more entered the political arena, initially as a civil service commissioner and then as Assistant Secretary of the Navy. Roosevelt resigned in 1898 to fight in the Spanish-American War, in which he made his name with the "Rough Riders". His popularity ensured his election as Governor of New York, but local party bosses were unhappy and in 1900 maneuvred him into the vice-presidency. With the death of McKinley, Roosevelt became president. His main platforms were enforcement of anti-trust legislation, wilderness conservation, the regulation of the railways, the prohibition of adulterated food, drugs and drinks, and an expansionist but far-sighted internationalism. In this last respect he recognized the new republic of Panama, which made possible the building of the Panama Canal to a scheme pioneered by McKinley.

In the 1904 election he defeated the Democrat Alton B. Parker by 336 Electoral College votes to 140, and continued the policies of his first administration. Roosevelt refused re-nomination in 1909.

Birthplace	Cincinnati, Ohio
Date of birth	15 September 1857
Education	Yale
Profession	Lawyer
Presidential term	4 March 1909 to 4 March 1913
Party	Republican
Place of death	Washington, D.C.
Date of death	8 March 1930
Place of burial	Arlington National Cemetery, Washington, D.C.

William H. Taft
27th President

The main distinction of William H. Taft was perhaps the fact that he weighed more than any other president. In other respects, he was a mediocre performer who tried unsuccessfully to take over from the lead set by Roosevelt. Taft was born into a powerful political family, and after proving himself an able lawyer, he turned to politics as a matter of course. His first appointments were in administrative fields, and with Roosevelt's backing he was nominated as the Republican candidate for the 1908 election, which he won with 321 Electoral College votes to Democrat William J. Bryan's 162. Taft adhered to "Rooseveltian" policies, though with a sounder legal basis for his activities. However in 1912 Roosevelt ran against him for the nomination, and with this division between the Republicans evident, Taft and Roosevelt lost to the democrat Woodrow Wilson.

A 1908 electioneering plate for the Republicans offers the presidential and vice-presidential running mates surrounded by luminaries of the "Grand Old Party" between 1856 and 1908.

Woodrow Wilson
28th President

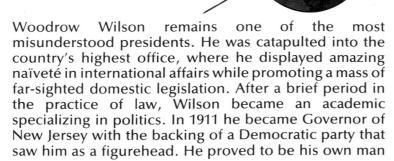

Woodrow Wilson remains one of the most misunderstood presidents. He was catapulted into the country's highest office, where he displayed amazing naïveté in international affairs while promoting a mass of far-sighted domestic legislation. After a brief period in the practice of law, Wilson became an academic specializing in politics. In 1911 he became Governor of New Jersey with the backing of a Democratic party that saw him as a figurehead. He proved to be his own man and in 1912 became the party's nominee for president. The Republican vote was hopelessly split between Taft and Roosevelt, allowing Wilson to win with 435 Electoral College votes to his opponents' 88 and 8. Wilson steered the United States through the First World War. He also established a central banking system, improved anti-trust measures, limited child labor, provided compensation for federal workers, and supported the 19th Amendment giving the vote to women. In 1916 he was re-elected with 277 votes to Charles E. Hughes's 254, but his last years were marred by illness.

Birthplace	Staunton, Virginia
Date of birth	28 December 1856
Education	Harvard and Columbia
Profession	Teacher
Presidential term	4 March 1913 to 4 March 1921
Party	Democrat
Place of death	Washington, D.C.
Date of death	3 February 1924
Place of burial	Washington, D.C.

On 2 April 1917 Woodrow Wilson appeared before the assembled congressmen and senators to ask for an American declaration of war against Germany.

Birthplace	Blooming Grove (now Corsica), Ohio
Date of birth	2 November 1865
Education	Ohio Central College
Profession	Journalist
Presidential term	4 March 1921 to 2 August 1923
Party	Republican
Place of death	San Francisco, California
Date of death	2 August 1923
Place of burial	Marion, Ohio

Warren Harding
29th President

By general consensus, Warren Harding was the worst president. Admired and even loved right up to the time he died in office, he was then revealed to have presided over an administration of quite extraordinary corruption. After failing to qualify as a lawyer, Harding became a newspaper man and then rose through the ranks of the Republican machine in Ohio. In 1914 he became a U.S. senator, and in 1920 he was chosen as the Republican presidential nominee when the party convention was deadlocked. Harding campaigned for a "return to normality", and defeated his Democrat opponent, James M. Cox, by a handsome 404 Electoral College votes to 127. The Harding administration was notable for the ascendancy of big business and the U.S. repudiation of the League of Nations promoted by Wilson. Harding died of a stroke while returning from a trip to Alaska.

A Ku Klux Klan march in Washington typified the relaxation of moral standards during the Harding administration of the early 1920s.

41

Calvin Coolidge
30th President

It is a beautiful irony that the United States should have had as president during most of the "Roaring '20s" a taciturn and even puritanical New Englander, Calvin Coolidge. Coolidge rose through the Republican machine in Massachusetts, and his firm handling of the Boston police strike of 1919 secured his nomination as vice-presidential running mate to Harding. With Harding's death Coolidge became president, and his first task was to root out the corruption attendant on Harding's presidency. Following a firmly conservative line, he kept the presidency in the 1924 election with 382 Electoral College votes to the Democrat John W. Davis's 136 and the Progressive Robert M. LaFollette's 13. Coolidge's administration was notable for its economy and laissez-faire. Its main failings were its inability to deal with gangsterism. In 1928 Coolidge refused re-nomination.

Birthplace	Plymouth, Vermont
Date of birth	4 July 1872
Education	Amherst College
Profession	Lawyer
Presidential term	3 August 1923 to 4 March 1929
Party	Republican
Place of death	Northampton, Massachusetts
Date of death	5 January 1933
Place of burial	Plymouth, Vermont

The era of prohibition under Coolidge was notable for the enormous rise of gangsterism, now best known for the bootlegging of alcohol and the official efforts to halt the trade.

Hoover's presidency is best remembered today as the time of the "Great Crash" and the devastating depression that followed in its wake.

Herbert Hoover
31st President

A mining engineer who became a self-made millionaire, Herbert Hoover became involved in government as an administrator in the distribution of relief to Belgium and northern France in the First World War. Between 1921 and 1928 Hoover was Secretary of Commerce in the Harding and Coolidge administrations. Hoover was nominated to succeed Coolidge, and riding on the popularity of his predecessor, he was elected with 444 Electoral College votes to the Democrat Alfred E. Smith's 87. But shortly after Hoover took office the "Great Crash" occurred. The president was faced with the problem of restoring the country. Some advised government intervention, while others argued that the economy should be left to resolve itself, and Hoover, still the astute businessman, chose a middle course of limited government intervention combined with economic confidence-building. Re-nominated in 1932, Hoover lost the election to Roosevelt. With ten million people unemployed, the country blamed him for the Depression following the crash. He retired to California.

Birthplace	West Branch, Iowa
Date of birth	10 August 1874
Education	Stanford University
Profession	Mining engineer
Presidential term	4 March 1929 to 4 March 1933
Party	Republican
Place of death	New York, New York
Date of death	20 October 1964
Place of burial	West Branch, Iowa

43

Franklin D. Roosevelt

32nd President

[signature: Franklin D Roosevelt]

Birthplace	Hyde Park, New York
Date of birth	30 January 1882
Education	Harvard and Columbia
Profession	Lawyer
Presidential term	4 March 1933 to 12 April 1945
Party	Democrat
Place of death	Warm Springs, Georgia
Date of death	12 April 1945
Place of burial	Hyde Park, New York

The best U.S. president so far, Franklin Roosevelt presided over his country's emergence from the Depression, steered the nation through the Second World War, and was elected an unprecedented four times. In 1920 he was stricken by the polio that left him paralyzed from the waist down. In the election of 1933 he defeated the incumbent, Hoover, by 472 Electoral College votes to 59.

On taking office, Roosevelt swept into action with his "New Deal" legislation designed to restore the national economy. Employment boomed; this factor was largely responsible for Roosevelt's re-election in 1936. The second administration was marred by wrangling over Roosevelt's attempts to create a Supreme Court compliant to his policies, but the continuation of the "New Deal" policies ensured that he was re-elected again in 1940. Aware that the Second World War must inevitably reach the U.S., Roosevelt did much to overturn U.S. isolationism with the Lend-Lease Act, and after war did engulf the U.S. in December 1941, he

The event that brought Franklin Roosevelt's U.S. into World War II was the Japanese attack on the Pacific Fleet in Pearl Harbor during December 1941.

proved a great wartime leader. In 1944 Roosevelt was re-elected for a fourth term, but died shortly after his fourth inauguration.

44

Harry S Truman
33rd President

Birthplace	Independence, Missouri
Date of birth	8 May 1884
Education	Kansas City Law
Profession	Lawyer
Presidential term	12 April 1945 to 20 January 1953
Party	Democrat
Place of death	Kansas City, Missouri
Date of death	26 December 1972
Place of burial	Independence, Missouri

During World War II the U.S. became the most important of the Western Allies, and also the modern industrial giant that supplied much of the alliance's weapons and shipping.

Faced with the immense task of following Roosevelt in 1945, Harry Truman proved himself well able to meet the requirement and thus emerged as one of the best presidents. He decided on the use of the atomic bomb against Japan, brought the Second World War to a successful close, dealt with the initial problems of a post-war world, helped create the Marshall Plan and NATO, inaugurated the "Truman Doctrine" of U.S. support for nations fighting external aggression, and shaped the course of U.S.-Soviet relations in the initial days of the "Cold War" including the Korean War. Truman had fought in the First World War and after the failure of a commercial enterprise in the 1921 recession, he entered local politics as a Democrat, becoming a U.S. senator in 1935. In 1944 he was chosen as Roosevelt's vice-presidential running mate, and became president in 1945. He was re-elected in 1948 with 303 Electoral College votes to the 189 and 39 won by the Republican Thomas E. Dewey and States Rights J. Strom Thurmond respectively. Truman refused re-nomination in 1952.

Dwight D. Eisenhower

34th President

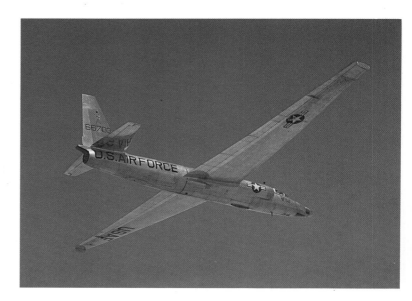

Under the Eisenhower administration the U.S. became greatly concerned with the U.S.S.R.'s emergence as a nuclear power, and developed machines such as this Lockheed U-2 to keep tabs on Soviet developments.

The presidency of Dwight D. Eisenhower was not notable for important legislation or reform, but was important for its moral impact: the United States created by the "Eisenhower years" is basically that which survives to the present. A career army officer, Eisenhower did not see service in the First World War but rose steadily in rank during the 1920s and 1930s. In the early 1940s, his masterly appreciation of strategic affairs commended him to General George C. Marshall, and Eisenhower progressed to Supreme Commander of the Allied forces fighting Germany. His military career continued after the Second World War, but in 1952 he resigned as NATO Supreme Commander in Europe to become the Republican presidential nominee. Eisenhower defeated the Democrat Adlai Stevenson with 442 Electoral College votes to 89, a defeat repeated in 1956 by 457 votes to 73 against the same opponent. Eisenhower sought with modest success to create a "new Republicanism" more aware of the need for social reform, but his presidency was marked by the McCarthy anti-communist hearings.

Birthplace	Denison, Texas
Date of birth	14 October 1890
Education	U.S. Military Academy, West Point
Profession	Soldier
Presidential term	20 January 1953 to 20 January 1961
Party	Republican
Place of death	Washington, D.C.
Date of death	28 March 1969
Place of burial	Abilene, Kansas

Birthplace	Brookline, Massachusetts
Date of birth	29 May 1917
Education	Princeton, Harvard, London School of Economics, and Stanford University
Profession	Author
Presidential term	20 January 1961 to 22 November 1963
Party	Democrat
Place of death	Dallas, Texas
Date of death	22 November 1963
Place of burial	Arlington National Cemetery, Washington, D.C.

John F. Kennedy
35th President

Kennedy and Soviet Premier Khrushchev met in Vienna in June 1961, the two leaders were deeply divided by Cold War issues.

John F. Kennedy was assassinated just short of his third anniversary in office. He was regarded at the time as one of the greatest presidents, largely as a result of his considerable civil rights legislation program, the creation of the Peace Corps and the bringing into the government structure of teachers, writers and scientists. However, hindsight has began to cast doubt on his basic morality and the skill with which he played the "Cold War" game: it was under Kennedy that there occurred the "Bay of Pigs" fiasco, the Cuban Missile Crisis and the U.S. entry to the Vietnam War. Born into a wealthy family, Kennedy served in the Second World War as a junior naval officer and later became a Democratic congressman. Rising to senatorial rank in 1958, he received the party's presidential nomination in 1960, winning the election with 300 Electoral College votes to Richard M. Nixon's 223. An international success was the Nuclear Test Ban Treaty, while his domestic program included tax reforms and better federal support for education and medicine.

47

Lyndon B. Johnson
36th President

American involvement in the Vietnam War reached its most massive and costly level during the years of the Johnson administration in the late 1960s.

Lyndon B. Johnson became president with the assassination of Kennedy, and his avowed intention was to create the type of country his predecessor had envisaged. Born into a southern farming family, Johnson flirted with teaching before entering public administration and, in 1937, he became a congressman. A significant political career followed, and in 1960 Johnson became Kennedy's vice-presidential running mate. He was elected in his own right in 1964, securing 486 Electoral College votes to the Republican Barry M. Goldwater's 52, and launched the "Great Society" to succeed Kennedy's "New Frontier". The dominant issues of Johnson's administration were the Vietnam War and civil rights. He remained committed to an anti-communist victory in Vietnam and thus fell foul of student-dominated unrest in the U.S. He was responsible for the furthest-reaching civil rights and social welfare legislation of any president after the Second World War. Broken by the vicissitudes of his administration, Johnson refused to stand for re-election in 1968.

Birthplace	Stonewall, Texas
Date of birth	27 August 1908
Education	Southwest Texas State Teachers College
Profession	Public administrator
Presidential term	22 November 1963 to 20 January 1969
Party	Democrat
Place of death	San Antonio, Texas
Date of death	22 January 1973
Place of burial	Johnson City, Texas

Birthplace	Yorba Linda, California
Date of birth	9 January 1913
Education	Whittier and Duke Universities
Profession	Lawyer
Presidential term	20 January 1969 to 9 August 1974
Party	Republican

Richard M. Nixon
37th President

John Kennedy's program to put a man on the Moon reached fruition in the Nixon presidency, and the full capability of American determination and technology were there for all to see.

Richard M. Nixon is best remembered as the first president to have resigned under threat of impeachment after the "Watergate Scandal" in which he connived at a break-in at the Democratic party headquarters. Yet a more realistic appraisal suggests that Nixon should be regarded as one of the better presidents, the man who extricated the U.S. from the Vietnam War and opened an era of detente (including the first Strategic Arms Limitation Treaty) with the communist powers after personal visits to Moscow and Beijing. After qualifying as a lawyer, Nixon served in the Second World War as a naval officer, and in 1946 became a congressman, who rose rapidly in stature with the McCarthy era of anti-communist purges. In 1950 he became a U.S. senator, and served as Eisenhower's vice-president between 1953 and 1961. He lost to Kennedy in the 1960 presidential election, but won in 1968 against the Democrat Hubert H. Humphrey with 301 Electoral College votes to 191, repeating the win in 1972 with 521 votes to 63 for his two opponents George McGovern and John Hosper.

Gerald R. Ford
38th President

Despite the propaganda highlighting the Vietnam War and its aftermath, Gerald Ford coped well with the task of restoring U.S. prestige after the battering it had received during the war.

Nixon's resignation led to the swearing-in of his vice-president, Gerald R. Ford, as the new president. The future president was born Leslie Lynch King, but his parents were divorced when he was two, and the boy was subsequently named after his mother's second husband. Though he was an extremely talented football player, the young Ford opted instead for the law. His budding career was overtaken by the Second World War, in which Ford served as a naval officer. After the war Ford chose a political career, and in 1948 he was elected a congressman. Thereafter Ford's career was good but undistinguished until 1973, when he was selected a vice-president by Nixon after the resignation of Spiro T. Agnew, disgraced on charges of graft and tax evasion. After the fall of Nixon, Ford was faced with the difficult task of restoring public confidence in the presidency. Ford played a key part in limiting the damage inflicted by the Arabs' 1973 oil embargo and subsequent price rise, but was narrowly defeated in the 1976 election.

Birthplace	Omaha, Nebraska
Date of birth	14 July 1913
Education	University of Michigan and Yale
Profession	Lawyer
Presidential term	9 August 1974 to 20 January 1977
Party	Republican

Birthplace	Plains, Georgia
Date of birth	1 October 1924
Education	U.S. Naval Academy, Annapolis, Maryland
Profession	Naval officer and farmer
Presidential term	20 January 1977 to 20 January 1981
Party	Democrat

James E. Carter
39th President

Flanked by Sadat of Egypt and Begin of Israel, "Jimmy" Carter signs the Camp David Agreement in which the U.S. helped end the constant threat of war between these two Middle Eastern neighbors.

The 1976 election of "Jimmy" Carter proved that voters had not been placated by Ford's damage-control measures after the disgraces of Agnew and Nixon. They voted for a politician who had never concerned himself with national, let alone international, affairs. Carter was elected with 297 Electoral College votes to Ford's 241. Carter's childhood ambition was to join the navy, but he resigned after eight years to look after the family farming business when his father died. It prospered, and Carter entered local politics to become Governor of Georgia. Largely unknown when he became the Democrats' 1976 nominee, solid support from southern blacks as well as whites gave him the election by a narrow margin. Carter's domestic policy of civil rights and social reform was partially lost to a hostile Congress, but foreign policy achievements were further detente with the U.S.S.R. and the Camp David Agreement between Israel and Egypt. The failure of the Tehran hostage mission turned voters against him, and Carter lost the 1980 election.

Ronald Reagan
40th President

Ronald Reagan (signature)

After acting in 54 films and becoming increasingly involved in conservative politics and causes, Ronald Reagan turned to active politics and was elected Governor of California in 1966. He was re-elected in 1970, but had his sights set firmly on greater things. After losing the 1976 Republican presidential nomination to Ford, in 1980 he secured the nomination and skilfully used the aftermath of the Iran hostages fiasco to trounce Carter with 489 Electoral College votes to 49, thereby becoming the oldest man ever elected president. He repeated the performance in 1984 when he defeated Walter Mondale by 525 votes to 13. After two terms as President, Reagan left office in 1989. The law now limits presidents to a maximum of two terms, he is believed to be considering a campaign to remove this stricture. The Reagan administration was notable for its comparative neglect of social affairs on the U.S. domestic level in favor of strengthening the international position of the U.S. This was achieved through a toughening of the U.S. stance on a host of international issues such as terrorism

On 28 May 1984 President Reagan lays a wreath at the Tomb of the Unknown Serviceman of the Vietnam War at Arlington National Cemetery. With events such as this the wounds of this dire war began slowly to close in the U.S.

The Reagan administration saw the renaissance of the U.S. space program with the advent of the space shuttle, and then its temporary extinction after the explosion that destroyed Challenger *and her crew.*

Birthplace	Tampico, Illinois
Date of birth	6 February 1911
Education	Eureka College
Profession	Actor
Presidential term	20 January 1981 to 20 January 1989
Party	Republican

and the need for a concerted Western stance against communist politico-military maneuvrings. This toughening also embraced a considerable boost in U.S. defense spending, partly on so-called conventional weapons but increasingly on the "Strategic Defense Initiative" pushed through an increasingly hostile Congress. Despite the embarrassment of the so-called "Irangate" scandal involving the illegal sales of weapons to Iran and the diversion of the profits to aid the Contra rebels fighting the communist government of Nicaragua, Reagan maintained a high level of personal popularity, and will certainly be remembered as the president responsible for so markedly improving U.S. relations with China and, more particularly, the U.S.S.R., capitalizing on the advent to power of a new breed of communist leader but treating with them from a position of political and military strength. In the longer term Reagan may come in for criticism for his neglect of the economic considerations that have saddled the U.S. with a monumental international trade deficit.

George Bush
41st President

Birthplace	Milton, Massachusetts
Date of birth	12 June 1924
Education	Yale University
Profession	Oil industrialist
Presidential term	20 January 1989 to
Party	Republican

George Bush served two terms as Reagan's vice-president before securing the 1988 Republican presidential nomination. In the election he soundly defeated the Democrat Michael Dukakis. Bush embarked on a career in the Texas oil industry after the Second World War, in which he had a distinguished career as a pilot. In 1967 he entered national politics when he was elected to Congress. He was twice defeated in his efforts to become a U.S. senator, becoming instead the U.S. Ambassador to China. It was during this time that U.S. detente with China was initiated, and in 1980 Bush was chosen as Reagan's vice-presidential running mate. Since the beginning of his presidency there have been extraordinary changes in the balance of world power in which Bush has played a leading role.

On the campaign trail. George and Barbara Bush meet Mickey and friends at Disneyland.